I Thank God

written by Marie Frost
illustrated by Kathryn Hutton

© 1986, The STANDARD PUBLISHING Company, Cincinnati, Ohio
Division of STANDEX INTERNATIONAL Corporation. Printed in Italy.

Thank You, God,
   For giving me
A quiet place
   Beneath a tree.

Why do you think Molly likes a quiet place?
Do you ever go to a quiet place where no one can bother you?
What do you do in your quiet place?

Thank You, God,
  For little things,
Like ladybugs
  And butterfly wings.

Point to the ladybug Molly is watching.
What is the butterfly doing?
What kind of bugs do you like to watch?

Thank You, God,
  For shining sun,
For grassy lawn
  Where my legs run.

Is Molly glad she has strong legs?
How can you tell?
What do you do with your strong legs?

Thank You, God,
   For the birds' nest.
You told the birds
   How to make it best.

Find the birds' nest hiding in the tree.
What is in the nest?
Should Molly touch the nest or the eggs?

Thank You, God,
 For my family—
Father, Mother,
 Brother, and me.

How many people are in Molly's family?
Can you name the people in your family?
Do you ever thank God for your family?

Thank You, God,
  For friends who say,
"I'll play with you,"
  And won't run away.

Do you think Molly shares with her friend?
Why do friends sometimes run off when
   you are playing with them?
Do you have a friend who always plays
   with you?

Thank You, God,
  That I can pray
Anyplace I go,
  And any time of day.

Where is Molly praying?
What do you think Molly is saying to God?
When do you talk to God?

Thank You, God,
 That I can say
Thank-you prayers
 On Thanksgiving Day.

What does your family do on Thanksgiving Day?
Do you say "Thank You" to God for all He does for you?
Can you say a thank-you prayer on other days?

Thank You, God,
  For signs of Spring,
For Easter time,
  When children sing.

Point to the things that tell Molly it is
   Spring.
Why do children sing at Easter time?
Why is Easter a happy time?

Have someone help you sing this thank-you song.

My Thank-You Song

Marie H. Frost Bonnie C. Hanson

1. I thank You, God, I thank You, God, Because You love me so. You made trees and pretty flowers grow.
2. I thank You, God, I thank You, God, For all the signs of Spring. You made Easter time when little children sing.
3. I thank You, God, I thank You, God, For all my family, Father, Mother, Brother, and there's me!